What's it like to be... a BUTTERFLY?

Jinny Johnson

illustrated by **Desiderio Sanzi**

W
FRANKLIN WATTS
LONDON • SYDNEY

An Appleseed Editions book

First published in 2013 by Franklin Watts
338 Euston Road, London NW1 3BH

© 2011 Appleseed Editions

Created by Appleseed Editions Ltd,
Well House, Friars Hill, Guestling,
East Sussex TN35 4ET

Designed and illustrated by Guy Callaby
Edited by Mary-Jane Wilkins

ISBN 978 1 4451 2189 5

Dewey Classification: 595.7'89

A CIP catalogue for this book is available
from the British Library.

Printed in China

Franklin Watts is a division of
Hachette Children's Books,
an Hachette UK company.
www.hachette.co.uk

Contents

4 Red admiral

6 Finding food

8 Starting life

16 Growing up

20 My first flight

22 More about butterflies

23 Butterfly words

24 Index

A butterfly is an insect.
It has six legs and two
pairs of colourful wings.

So what's it like to be a butterfly?

I love being a butterfly.

It's fun flying around
on my beautiful wings.

*I'm a special kind of butterfly
called a red admiral.*

Do you like my
red stripes and
white spots?

All day long I flutter from flower to flower.

I land on a flower and unroll my long tongue.

Red admiral butterflies also feed on juice from very ripe fruit.

Then I suck up a lovely sugary liquid called nectar.

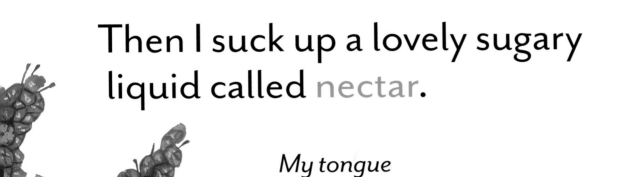

My tongue

Nectar is one of my favourite foods.

I didn't always
look like this.

I started life as a tiny egg.
My mum laid her eggs
on nettle leaves.

Can you see the tiny eggs she's laid?

I started to grow inside the egg.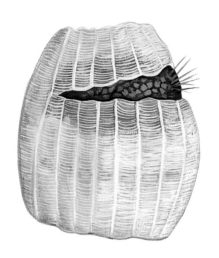

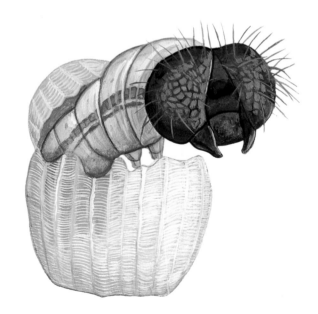

Then I made
a little hole
in the egg and
I wriggled out.

Look at me. I was a
creepy-crawly caterpillar.

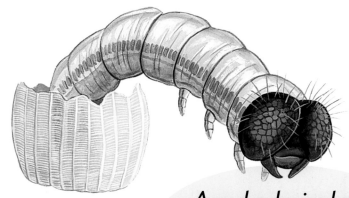

*A red admiral egg
hatches about a week
after it is laid.*

My mum wasn't there
when I hatched out.

But she knew
I would have
plenty to eat.

I gobbled up my eggshell after I'd hatched.

Then I began to eat as many nettle leaves as I could.

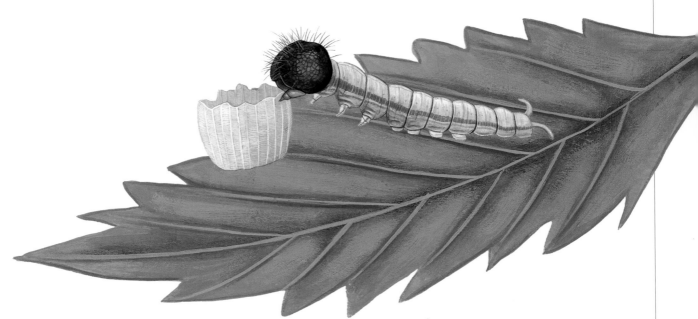

I was so busy eating it was hard to watch out for birds and spiders.

They sometimes catch and eat caterpillars like me.

So I found a big nettle leaf and folded it over myself.

I glued the edges together
with silk threads.

That kept
me safe.

*I made these silk
threads myself.*

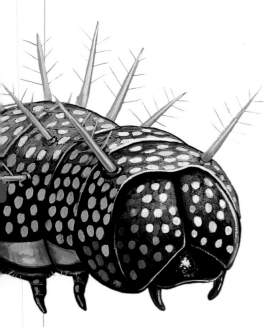

I ate so much I grew fatter and fatter.

My skin got very tight.

Most caterpillars shed their old skin four or five times as they grow.

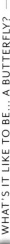

I had new skin growing underneath.

I wriggled out of my old skin and left it behind.

My old skin

This is my chrysalis.

When I had grown as big as I could, I stopped eating.

My skin split for the last time and underneath was a hard case called a chrysalis.

Inside this I turned from a caterpillar into a butterfly.

Then I wriggled out of the chrysalis.

I spread my wings and flew for the first time.

What fun that was.

Now I'm looking for another red admiral butterfly. We will mate and lay our own eggs.

Can you find another red admiral butterfly for me?

More about butterflies

Where do butterflies go in winter?

Butterflies don't like cold weather. Some fly to warmer places in winter. Others just find a sheltered spot and sleep all through the cold months.

What are butterfly wings made of?

Butterfly wings are made of tiny flat scales of different colours. These make up the patterns on the wings. The scales overlap slightly, like tiles on a roof.

How big are butterflies?

Most are a just a few centimetres across, but the biggest is the Queen Alexandra's birdwing butterfly. It is nearly 30 cm from wingtip to wingtip.

What does a butterfly use its feelers for?

A butterfly uses the two feelers, or antennae, on its head to smell things. The feelers also help the butterfly balance as it flies and perches.

Butterfly words

caterpillar
A creature that looks like a worm with legs. A butterfly spends the first part of its life as a caterpillar.

chrysalis
A hard case. A caterpillar changes into a butterfly inside a chrysalis.

mate
Male and female animals mate to produce young.

nectar
A sweet liquid inside flowers.

nettle
A kind of green plant.

silk
A fine, strong thread made by a caterpillar.

Butterfly index

caterpillar 11, 13, 14, 15, 16, 17, 18, 19, 23
chrysalis 18, 19, 23

egg 9, 10, 11, 13, 21

feelers 22
flowers 6, 7

nectar 7, 23
nettles 9, 13, 14, 23

silk 15, 23
skin 16, 17

tongue 6, 7

wings 3, 5, 20, 22